# Raising Special Kids

## A Group Program for Parents of Children with Special Needs

### Facilitator's Manual

Jared D. Massanari

Alice E. Massanari

Research Press ○ 2612 North Mattis Avenue ○ Champaign, Illinois 61822 ○ (800) 519-2707
www.researchpress.com

Copies of this book and the *Parent Guidebook* for this program may be ordered from Research Press at the address given on the title page.

Composition by Jeff Helgesen
Cover design by Linda Brown, Positive I.D. Graphic Design, Inc.
Printed by United Graphics, Inc.

ISBN 13: 978-0-87822-552-1
Library of Congress Control Number 2007939445

# CONTENTS

# ACKNOWLEDGMENTS

A parenting program such as *Raising Special Kids* could not be produced without the assistance of many talented and generous people. During the years we have used this program, we have consulted with many skillful professionals to help us create and disseminate this material. The guidance and expertise of Research Press have made publication of this version possible.

In addition to this technical assistance, we have learned much from all of the parents we have been fortunate enough to meet while conducting this program. Their stories have inspired and supported this project.

Finally, we would like to thank our own parents, who taught us much from their example, and our two children, Caleb and Adrienne, who continue to present us with endless opportunities to become conscious parents.

# IMPLEMENTING THE PROGRAM

## OVERVIEW

We have written the *Raising Special Kids* program to address directly the responsibilities and expectations faced by parents raising children with special needs, whether these needs are physical, cognitive, emotional, or behavioral. Many excellent resources are available to parents raising children with special needs. Many effective parenting classes are offered in communities. But because we know firsthand the intense feelings that accompany parenting a special child, we are convinced that a program for parents of children with special needs must begin by focusing parents on the emotional experience of raising their child. This program applies what we know about parenting in general to the special circumstances faced by parents raising children with special needs.

Frequently, families raising a child with special needs feel isolated from other families, disconnected from each other, and overwhelmed by their experiences without knowing how to understand what is happening or having the skills to manage what is occurring. *Raising Special Kids* is designed to assist families by connecting them with other families in the community, by encouraging them to spend time together as a family, by providing perspectives on their emotional experience that can lead to acceptance and empowerment, and by helping them understand the goals of healthy, conscious parenting.

This program is based on principles of parenting expressed in most current parenting materials. These principles are summarized as follows:

1. A problem or success for a family member affects everyone in the family.

2. Adults have a responsibility to attend to their own needs; children should not be expected to meet the needs of adults. (Remember the directive from airline attendants: "In case of an emergency, put on your own oxygen mask first, then assist your child.")

3. The parental role often evokes unresolved issues from adults' own childhood, and these issues may interfere with the appropriate application of parenting skills.

4. Parents have at least two primary functions: One is to provide a nurturing environment; the other is to promote growth of the individual child toward autonomy.

5. Children who take responsibility for themselves are children who have been allowed to make mistakes and learn from the consequences without criticism.

6. Children learn from what parents do more than from what they say. Changing a child's behavior requires that parents become more conscious of and alter their own behaviors.

7. Children cannot progress in their emotional growth any faster than their parents do.

8. A child communicates through behavior that expresses his or her feelings. If a parent desires a change in a child's behavior, the parent must learn to validate the feelings motivating the behavior of the child.

9. Acceptance, approval, respect, and encouragement are more powerful motivators for change in children than disapproval, punishment, and control.

The goal of this program is to assist parents in becoming *conscious parents* by applying these principles in their own families. In the process of using these principles, parents will develop the following skills:

► Recognizing personal history and its impact on the role of a parent who is identifying and expressing personal feelings

► Observing and establishing boundaries that distinguish parent from child

► Processing loss and tolerating pain

► Recognizing unfulfilled dreams and expectations for oneself and one's child

► Identifying developmental needs of the child that can be met within the limits of the child's abilities

► Developing self-soothing behaviors, such as taking time for oneself and adult relationships, sharing with others to foster support, and discovering a sense of humor

► Trusting other people and other systems

While all of these skills are helpful in any parenting situation, they are essential for parents raising children with special needs.

In this program, we explore issues common to the experience of parents raising children with a variety of special needs. Our purpose is to provide information that may be applied to meet the needs of a range of individual circumstances, but our main interest is in helping parents discover what is similar about their parenting experience, not in identifying what is different.

## PROGRAM METHODS

In this program, we map out suggested routes and destinations for parents. This map is based on our personal and professional experience, as well as on the insights of other theoreticians and educators. Most parents are already familiar with the story "Welcome to Holland," and we use it as a focus of discussion throughout the sessions. This story, written in 1987 by Emily Perl Kingsley about the experience of living with her son Jason, born with Down syndrome, has been translated into numerous languages and published on scores of Web sites. In it, a traveler who has planned and dreamed about a visit to Italy unexpectedly lands in Holland. The parents of a child with special needs share many of the emotions the traveler feels: shock, dismay, anger, sadness, betrayal, and fear. In addition to learning how to manage these intense feelings without being overwhelmed, parents are now challenged to make decisions that affect their child. And all of this in a foreign land! The skills required are very demanding.

As a facilitator and tour guide for your group, you will be required to acknowledge and support a variety of approaches to life experiences, as well as a variety of parenting methods. Differing perspectives generate lively conversation and discourse. Our theoretical foundation will become apparent as you follow the group's direction. We do ask that you conduct the sessions in the order they are presented. We feel the progression of issues parents need to explore is critical to their developing the skills required to parent children with special needs.

On our trip to Holland, we develop a number of theories. We expand some more fully than others; all are vital to the complex interaction of parent and child. We invite you to consider the following themes as you move through the curriculum.

## The Dance between Parent and Child

Imagine the interplay between parent and child as a dance, a wonderfully complex movement of forces. Each of the dancers is pulled by the desire to attach, and each is pushed to individuate. Pulled together; pushed apart. Like magnets, each of the dancers has both poles. At times, parent and child are attracted to each other; at other times, they find themselves separating. The trick, of course, is to know when to do each. We explore some of the challenges of this dance throughout the program, but especially in chapter 6 of the *Parent*

*Guidebook,* in the discussion of ages and stages of child development. Raising a child with special needs is an encounter with one of life's most challenging realities.

## The Need to Understand Losses

Second, we interpret parents' experience of raising a child with special needs as an encounter with one of life's most challenging questions: What do we each do when we do not get what we want? To ask this question with parents does not imply that they do not love or want their child. It does, however, mean that most parents begin their journey by planning and hoping for the birth of a healthy baby. With the birth or later discovery that the child has special needs, parents are inevitably faced with the question of what they think and feel about not getting the child they expected. Do they stay angry or pout, get depressed, feel victimized, or experience other difficult emotions? We have observed that how parents respond frequently reenacts what they learned as children growing up in their own families. And how parents act often impacts the way their children behave when they, in turn, do not get what they desire. Our goal in *Raising Special Kids* is to make families conscious of this process and, in the process, expand the choices possible.

We expand upon this process in our discussion of the expected child and expected parent, in chapter 2. We also develop this central theme by helping parents:

► Think about the child they expected
► Isolate the intense feelings that accompany loss
► Identify and express their emotional experience
► Become comfortable using the terms *grieving* and *chronic grieving* in order to normalize their experience
► Observe that the entire family has strong feelings about the experience of raising a child with special needs

## The Importance of Conscious Parenting

Throughout the program, we advocate that group members become conscious parents. The more parents know about themselves, their child, and the parent-child dance, the more likely the entire family will interact with respect, cooperation, and love. We identify conscious parents as parents who:

► Take care of themselves
► Learn to identify and encourage separation and attachment for each person in the family

- Advocate for the child's drive toward independence
- Identify and express their feelings
- Develop skills of listening to self and child
- Know how to step out of emotional reaction in order to design effective interventions for their child.
- Supplement research on the "special need" with information on normal child development
- Live in the present
- Enjoy life

Group experiences build on one another. As a result, toward the end of the program parents can more safely explore sensitive topics in depth. Group members will have discovered commonalities that will unite them and provide mutual support during discussion of more emotional experiences.

We hope you see this material as a structure that reflects true life experiences. A map is never the same thing as an actual experience. It may point the way. It may make the journey a little less chaotic. It may even alert us to what is coming. But a map will not, and should not, replace the experience itself. You will find side roads and paths off the road that need to be taken by a specific group within a particular session. The quality of the journey is as important as reaching the final destination.

This curriculum may need to be adapted for particular groups to address cultural differences. Our frame of reference is middle-class experience, and we recognize this limitation. While the program's underlying premises are central to human experience, you may need to use a different language to apply them. Let your own experience with other cultures help you find ways to bring this material alive.

## YOUR ROLE AS A FACILITATOR

We feel that the most effective facilitators are those who know this material from personal experience. For us, the key to having a solid understanding of this material is having encountered losses in our own lives. Parents need to know that the facilitator has more than theoretical knowledge of this program. It is for this reason that we advocate having parent co-facilitators. With appropriate training and guidance, such parents can be a strong asset to the program.

We recommend that at least one of the facilitators be a mental health practitioner. The reason for this is that many tough and sometimes disturbing responses occur during the program. Sometimes parents verbalize thoughts or feelings that they have never expressed before. Couples may see their partners in a new light, and their new perceptions may bring up considerable fear, insecurity, and defensiveness. So it is vital that you, as the facilitator, know how to work with individuals who are in a state of distress. You need to know how to teach self-soothing skills to both individuals and families—and to recognize the need for skilled confrontation and provide it for parents whose denial and resistance to their feelings impede their ability to parent effectively.

We have provided you with a set of exercises and specific goals for each session's theme. These tools will focus the work for each session. They will also give participants ample opportunity to share with one another. Your direction is vital to the flow of each session. Calm, yet firm, leadership will keep participants on task. Following the structure will also give your group a sense of security as emotional issues arise and are addressed.

As you get to know the group you are working with, we suggest that you focus on those activities that you think will be the most beneficial. Sessions have been written in such depth that it may be difficult to complete each exercise within the time available. You may need to summarize and condense some of the material in order to keep moving through the entire program. You will also need to encourage parents to prepare for upcoming sessions so that group time can be used efficiently.

To support your role as a facilitator, we offer some general principles that apply to most psychoeducational groups:

1. Refer problems back to the group. Facilitators should remain focused primarily on parenting principles and ask the group to advise one another on how best to apply them. Group input reduces the possibility that facilitators will be blamed for attempted changes that fall short of anticipated results. It also tends to equalize group participation and prevent an imbalance of focus on one or two participants.

2. Remember that this process may expose problems that must be addressed outside the group. For example, if issues of domestic violence or chemical abuse within a family surface, use a clinical approach to remind the parents that parenting issues cannot be successfully resolved until they deal with those adult problems. Their skills in parenting cannot advance beyond their skills in relating to themselves or to one another. Likewise, participation in this group will probably expose some situations in which a parent functions with a significant psychological problem. When possible, encourage parents to find creative ways to work together to solve problems. Do not hesitate, if necessary, to suggest privately that they seek individual or family therapy. This is not a therapy group, but it can be viewed as a wonderful opportunity

to engage parents in self-reflection and to point the way for more intense interventions when necessary.

3. Keep a list of other resource agencies and programs readily available and encourage parents to share their findings about support systems with one another. Do not, however, let the group focus on this type of interaction during sessions, or it will become a support or information exchange group that focuses on advice giving. The goal is to assist parents in learning to problem-solve for themselves, not to foster dependency. Keep the group focused on emotional process rather than on situational content. This can be tough!

4. Stay flexible and exercise your own creativity. When your group appears stuck, try something new. If one person is dominating, suggest an art activity that is done individually, then shared in a "round." Be sure to ask for responses from parents who may be quieter; allow time without pressure. Do not allow the group to focus repeatedly on one specific problem or on one particular family. Keep the group needs in mind.

5. Share your personal experiences. Participate in group self-disclosure, but keep your comments brief and to the point. As a facilitator, you are an experienced guide for a community on a path you are exploring together, not shepherds or entertainers.

6. Tune in to humor. We aspire to group laughter a few times a session, not as a means of avoidance but to provide balance and to promote the feeling of belonging. Many families feel embarrassed by the situations they laugh about, but laughing relieves tension. Deep connections can be formed when they laugh together. Expect some macabre humor; in proper dosage, it's very healing.

7. Don't panic about silence and initial nonparticipation. It doesn't necessarily mean that the group is resistant. It may take as many as four or five sessions for some members to feel safe participating. Some participants are very involved internally but are not ready to verbalize in what may be a totally new arena.

8. Gracefully acknowledge your own mistakes. In many ways, facilitators model appropriate parenting to their groups. Some of the same skills come into play. Most of us need to be supported in the belief that learning occurs when we feel free to risk making mistakes.

## GROUP PROCESS

As already stated, many excellent parenting curricula are now available. A good number are structured for groups, and many require trained and even certified teachers. But these programs may over-look a central component of the experience of parenting children with special needs; that is, the fact that parents are not getting what they anticipated. At the core of parenting children with special needs is the parents' need to let go of the "expected child." This parenting process is about loss, and, as we know, grieving is about intense and sometimes overwhelming feelings of anger, sadness, despair, guilt, and fear.

The parents gathered in this group will frequently be involved with deep emotions and be in the midst of asking very tough questions. They may be in considerable pain, suffering not only from their own losses but also from their daily engagement with a child who may be in both emotional and physical pain. Many times, these parents are confronting systems—educational, medical, social—that move only with pressure and time. We have found that many parents are angry and tired. They are frustrated and want assistance. Yet some-times they don't know how to trust or whom to trust. Most of them have had little encouragement in handling their own feelings and may feel selfish doing so or may not even be aware of the depth of their feelings. They can create a very emotionally demanding group.

We have found that parents are eager to learn. They desire a forum in which to share their stories. In fact, much of the interaction in such groups resembles storytelling, with one person talking and the others listening, then another, then another. When given permis-sion to feel—which is the essence of this program—parents will eagerly share what life has brought them.

Your work is easy in one sense—just give parents permission and ask specific questions, and they will be off and running! Yet in another way your task is difficult, for not everyone moves at the same pace. Much of your work will be that indescribable phenomenon of managing group process. You will need to quiet some individuals without shaming or judging; you will need to encourage others without rescuing them. You will need to provide just the right amount of information with the appropriate leeway for each participant to integrate the material in his or her own way. It is the challenging work of listening, telling, and rewriting life stories so that everyone, including you, feels heard.

## ORGANIZATION OF PARENTS' AND CHILDREN'S GROUPS

Participants can be gathered from a variety of sources. For example, this program can focus on a population that uses medical resources or be offered in a hospital setting. We have collaborated with an agency serving families with children who have chronic illnesses as well as a child development program and a Family Services America agency. Many of our families have been reached through school systems, particularly through contacts with a variety of special education programs. The schools have been generous in providing space for groups to meet. Other contacts have come from hospital pediatric units or neonatal intensive care units and from special-focus health care groups such as rehabilitation programs, pediatric physician groups, cystic fibrosis and cerebral palsy support groups, and diabetes treatment programs. This program serves well as a basis for collaboration among agencies that in turn support successful grant proposals.

We have found that the parent group operates most effectively when a concurrent group is provided for children. This service should not be viewed as baby-sitting; we are convinced that equally well-trained and sensitive leaders are vital for the children's group. If you provide a children's group, make sure that the children are offered enjoyable and enriching activities so that they want to be a part of the meetings. Their motivation often keeps parents coming in the face of otherwise discouraging scheduling problems or personal anxiety about participating.

We recommend including all the children from a family in the children's group. Sometimes parents' work focuses as much on difficulties with siblings of the child with special needs, so it is a good idea to have all family members involved in the program. In fact, we consider this program to be a family one, which means that anyone who is considered part of the family is invited to participate.

Sufficient staff must be available to ensure a safe place for the children, and competent leaders must provide a program that is engaging to them. Only then will parents feel comfortable spending time in their own group, separate from their children.

If the leaders of the children's group are well trained and positive about their experience with the group, they can prove to be an invaluable resource for your program. Much of the approach of this curriculum builds on the fact that parents are stuck in seeing their child in only one way. When other adults and children perceive and interact with the child in new ways, parents may be more able to acknowledge that part of the problems in the family originate with their own perceptions. This shift in perceptions allows parents to be more hopeful that change is possible, even within limitations.

We have benefited enormously from the participation of such a children's group facilitator. During our seventh session, the facilitator visits the parents' group for 30 minutes to provide a very encouraging perspective on each of the children. Often the facilitator views the children as having a much greater capacity for independence and emotional development than the parents had realized.

We like to have parents and children meet in different parts of a building or in two separate buildings so that noise does not distract either group and neither parent nor child is tempted to seek out the other to resolve a problem. This is a time for the family to be separated and to learn that everything is all right. Parents and children can be away from one another for two hours, mother and father can spend quality time with each other separate from the children, and both can learn and have fun without the other. These assumptions may sound elementary, but don't overlook the fact that for many of these families, separation is frequently accompanied by intense fear and anxiety. You may need to create some transitional experiences for such families. In general, just remember that the two groups should foster trust for both children and parents by providing the children with safe and responsible caretakers.

Time and place should be the same for both group's meetings. We recommend scheduling the groups in successive weekly sessions, with two hours set aside for each meeting. Most of our groups have met in the early evening (from 6:00 to 8:00 P.M.), to accommodate working parents as well as early bedtimes for children. Evening sessions also make it less likely that one parent will use work as an excuse to avoid attending.

We have run this program on a 90-minute weekly format, which works well for the children's group but is not as satisfactory for the parents' sessions. Two hours is much better. Whatever is decided about the meeting time, it is essential that the parents' and children's groups end as scheduled.

We suggest that you have art materials (paper, colored markers, crayons, pencils, tape, etc.) as well as an easel pad or dry erase board and VCR or DVD player available each evening in the parents' group. We like to arrange the parents' chairs in a circle, which gives the group a sense of unity and equality. Other than for art projects, avoid tables, as they create communication barriers in this type of group.

Ideally, 12 to 16 individuals can be registered for the parents' group. Expect two to four individuals to drop out when they encounter group challenges or when the inevitable health care crises of their children demand their attention elsewhere. Couples should be encouraged to come together; single-parent families are also welcome. Two facilitators can present, monitor, and process the group more comfortably and thoroughly than one can. A children's group will demand more staff than the parents' group if the same number of children attend. Creative arrangements can be made, however, to accommodate the needs of the particular families that choose to participate in the program.

Your children's group will need to be planned by someone who truly understands the meaning of the phrase "children with special needs." During the screening and registration process, be sure to identify these needs as well as the ages and any other special requirements for all children expected to attend.

We have found it best to close the program to new families after the second meeting because latecomers disrupt the development of trust within the group. During the screening and registration process, be sure to emphasize that families should plan to attend all sessions, not just those on topics of interest. As is the case for all groups, there will be some early attrition, so you can plan to register a few more participants than may be ideal.

Many times, the parents and children will lobby at the end of the program experience for the sessions to continue. We feel that ending the group formally is vital. Much that we explore together is about being able to say good-bye consciously and directly. Even if the families want to gather informally after the program concludes, we strongly recommend that everyone recognize the group sessions you provide as a time-limited experience in which all will share the process of saying good-bye.

## SUPPLEMENTAL RESOURCES

We recommend using audiovisual materials during the program, as time permits. Although the group sessions can be offered without such resources, we have found that these materials provide parents with important information and valuable insights and do so with an emotional impact not easily obtained from other resources. We have used feature films, readily available on videotape or DVD, to good effect. Some excellent examples include *Lorenzo's Oil, Ordinary People, Dead Poets Society, The Patty Duke Story, Brian's Song, Elephant Man, The Miracle Worker, Resurrection, My Left Foot, The Horse Whisperer, Kramer versus Kramer,* and *Miracle in Lane 2.*

In addition, songs and selections of music can enliven the group. Children's books can be used to demonstrate new and exciting ways to discuss issues with children. For other helpful ideas, consult the links on our Web site at www.interactivefamilyresources.com. Feel free to supplement this material with your own ideas. Find a balance in using outside resources to generate participation.

## USING ART ACTIVITIES

A few of the exercises in this program require using art materials. The value of art activities—regardless of the person's skill level—is that they can lower certain intellectual defenses that adults use against talking about feelings. You can expect some participants to respond to the request to draw a picture with the rejoinder, "Oh, I can't draw." It will be important that you, as the group leader, reassure your participants that these exercises are not supposed to produce great art. Simply restate the assignment and encourage each person to enjoy the chance to respond to a parenting issue in a new way.

Invite each participant to have fun with it in the way a child would. Point out that you are not looking for a particular kind of art product; rather, you are using the art materials to give each person a chance to express a particular experience nonverbally. Remind parents that their anxiety about trying something new is akin to the feelings a child may have about learning a new skill. Suggest that parents refrain from interacting with one another until art projects are completed to avoid becoming distracted by responses to their work or by their own interest in someone else's.

You will strengthen your credibility and lower group anxiety by participating in art activities and sharing your own artwork. Our premise is that facilitators should never ask group members to participate in an activity that they themselves would be unwilling to do. Such participation again underscores the need for facilitators to be comfortable with the way they have processed their own feelings of loss and pain before asking others to do so.

Equally important as the individual's response to the drawing activity is the way the group discusses each person's pictures. We begin by having participants place their artwork on the floor in front of them, facing the circle. Then we ask one parent to volunteer to tell us about his or her drawing, continuing around the circle until everyone has had a chance to contribute. Sharing pictures can be a very touching and intimate experience. Group interaction is not art criticism. Drawings are to be treated with the same kind of respect with which we treat people. Questions, of course, can be asked, and clarifications can also be requested. It is inappropriate, however, to make derogatory comments about one's own or another's drawing. Modeling curiosity and excitement for the group will go a long way toward helping group members benefit from these activities. We have found the art experiences to be some of the most gratifying in our groups because they deepen personal awareness and group cohesion.

Some suggested activities in the program require families to make drawings together. Art offers the family an exercise that all members can participate in equally (unless, of course, a child with special needs is unable to join in, which means the family will need to experiment with other activities). Whereas verbal expression may limit children, art tends to equalize the playing field. The parents' experience with these activities in the group will open them to facilitating similar experiences at home.

The art materials required are minimal. We use paper of various sizes; newsprint works well and is inexpensive. We also use different kinds of crayons, colored markers, pencils, pens, and pastels. Sometimes we assign a collage, so all kinds of materials can be made available: old magazines, glitter, glue, ribbons, flowers, twigs, clay, and so forth. The simplest supplies are often the best. Don't forget to bring plenty of scissors as well as enough supplies for each participant to choose whatever art material he or she prefers.

## USING INTERACTIVE FAMILY ACTIVITIES

Two kinds of tasks are provided for the parent during this program. First, we ask that parents come prepared to discuss the material in the Parent Guidebook. This requires reading the material in the guidebook for the assigned session and answering the questions, which will be discussed in group. Second, we ask that parents complete the activities at the end of each chapter that you assign or alternative activities, if you wish to suggest them. These simple assignments give families a chance to practice some of the ideas discussed. The exercises are frequently family based and can provide excellent material for exploration at the following session.

Families may substitute another activity for the ones suggested in their guidebook. The activity, however, should not focus on a type of "entertainment." For example, putting together a jigsaw puzzle or planning and having a picnic together might be appropriate, but a trip to a museum, although a terrific family activity, would not meet the goals of the assignment. Parents are encouraged to find ways for the family to be together that focus on the family itself, not on some external stimulation or entertainment.

Not every participant will do the homework. We have found that the best way to proceed is to begin each meeting with a time-limited exploration of how the suggested reading and activities went. This will encourage parents to complete their tasks. It also communicates the message that the activities are chosen to encourage family involvement, a message that will deepen parents' participation in the program.

We leave it up to you to decide how to confront the issue of not completing the preparatory work. Our experience has been that it is helpful to state that maximum program benefits result only when each parent thinks about and practices the ideas being explored during the time between groups. Learning can occur without any preparation by parents, but this new learning has a better chance to impact the entire family if parents complete the reading and activities. When the family works together outside the sessions, it also reinforces positive change.

When the preparation is completed outside of meetings, facilitators have a great deal more freedom about which material to focus on during the group session. As mentioned previously, you may not be able to complete all the activities. Your own preview of each session and sensitivity to the needs of your particular group will help you in synthesizing material for group discussion.

## GROUP GUIDELINES

We recommend that the first session include establishing a few group rules. Ask for suggestions from the participants, or use a version of the guidelines that appear on the next page. Make sure everyone understands that the agreed-upon rules apply to each member of the group, including the facilitators.

## PRETEST-POSTTEST, PROGRAM EVALUATION, AND CERTIFICATE OF ATTENDANCE

To assess your group as well as your success as a facilitator and the program in general, we suggest that you administer the Pretest-Posttest (Appendix A) and have each parent complete the Program Evaluation form (Appendix B). We also recommend that you provide a Certificate of Attendance (Appendix C) on the last day your group meets. We recommend that parents do not miss more than two classes to remain eligible to receive a certificate. Other requirements for the completion of this program we leave to you.

The pretest-posttest is for informational and exploratory use with this curriculum. It is intended to assess attitudinal and behavioral changes in participants in order to provide feedback on the program's value to the participants and to the organizations sponsoring the program. It is a tool to determine whether the psycho-educational objectives of the curriculum have been met.

The pretest-posttest measures the following specific goals of the *Raising Special Kids* program:

► Improve connections with other families raising children with special needs

► Increase understanding of the emotional experience of parents raising children with special needs

► Gain awareness and understanding of the unique challenges of raising a child with special needs

► Improve family communication and skills of healthy parenting

► Increase general parenting satisfaction

Parents complete the test at the first meeting of the program and then retake the test at the last meeting. Change in specific areas can be quantified by comparing how parents respond to the same question before and after participation.

A more general observation about change can be demonstrated by totaling each parent's response to all questions and then comparing the total scores before and after participation. An effective program should result in an overall increase of scores on the posttest.

# Guidelines for the Raising Special Kids Group

In order to make this a challenging as well as safe place for you and others to learn, please follow these guidelines:

1. When you and others share your experiences, it is important to respect the person who is speaking.

   ► Listen as you would like to be listened to.

   ► Give others adequate time to express their thoughts and feelings. Limit your own speaking so that everyone gets a chance to talk.

   ► Silence is OK. Sometimes individuals need time to formulate their ideas and feelings.

   ► Tears and expressions of anger are acceptable.

   ► Empathy is more valuable than advice.

2. Whatever you or others say in the group stays in the group. We need to respect one another's confidences. The exception to this rule may be an occasion when your leaders need to discuss a situation with other colleagues, in which case permission to do so will be requested in advance.

3. You are free to "pass" on any experience you do not wish to share with other members of the group.

4. The group will begin and end on time.

From *Raising Special Kids: A Group Program for Parents of Children with Special Needs (Facilitator's Manual)*, by Jared D. Massanari and Alice E. Massanari, © 2008, Champaign, IL: Research Press (800-519-2707, www.researchpress.com)

# SESSION PLANS

# CHAPTER 1
# BECOMING A PARENT

## OBJECTIVES

1. Introduce families and facilitators to one another and begin to establish a level of comfort by appreciating their commitment to attend the program.
2. Develop group recognition of disappointment or sense of loss inherent in being the parent of a child with special needs.
3. Develop understanding of where we each learned how to be a parent.
4. Identify goals of parenting (the qualities parents hope their child will develop).
5. Identify desirable qualities and skills for parents.
6. Introduce the purpose of interactive family activities.

## MATERIALS

Name tags, pencils or pens

Easel pad or dry erase board

Copies of the Pretest-Posttest (Appendix A)

A copy of the *Parent Guidebook* for each group member

> *Note: Greet all participants as soon as they enter and have them fill in a name tag and any agency or organization registration forms necessary. You will want to obtain, at a minimum, name, address, phone number, and information regarding children, such as school, ages and developmental levels, special services, and so forth. Have each parent sign a name tag and complete the pretest.*

## INTRODUCTION

1. Introduce yourselves as the group facilitators, briefly describing your credentials, and make a brief statement about personal

experiences you have had with children with special needs, if applicable.

2. Ask participants to introduce themselves. They should include their first names and a brief introduction to their family, including names and ages of children, with a sentence or two describing the nature of the special needs.

   *Note: Limit these introductions while assuring the participants that the group will discuss their family situations in greater detail as the group progresses.*

3. Explain the nature of the group. It is important to communicate that the program is built on the belief that parents know their children best. Show appreciation for what they have already done for their children and make it clear that you want to learn about each family's experiences with their special child. Make sure the group understands that the focus will be on (a) where we are as parents now, (b) where we would like to be as parents, and (c) how to apply the tasks of parenting in a situation that includes a child with special needs. Encourage participants to share with one another before and after group meetings, especially on matters regarding available services, advocacy, and forming a support network.

   *Note: This will be the time to begin setting limits in order to maintain group focus. Some participants may want to use group time to vent frustrations with school, medical, or social services systems. Assure group members that they will have time to voice such concerns but that the focus of sessions will be on how to handle their feelings and the issues that arise with their children. If group members use the time only to vent frustrations with various systems or to exchange information, they may avoid the more difficult emotional issues.*

4. Introduce the idea of group guidelines (see page 15) and open the group for discussion on this subject so the members participate in establishing group rules. Write the group rules on the easel pad or dry erase board as participants approve them.

5. Give each parent a copy of the *Parent Guidebook* and explain that it includes readings and activities that form the basis for this and future sessions. Let the parents know that you will be working through some of the material from chapter 1 in this session.

## SESSION PLAN

1. Have participants turn to "Welcome to Holland" in the *Parent Guidebook* (p. 3). Begin reading the story aloud to the group. Stop

after "They've landed in Holland and there you must stay." Ask the group to name some of the feelings they would have about learning that they had landed in Holland when they anticipated landing in Italy. They will instinctively apply this to the notion of having a child with special needs.

- List these feelings.
- Finish reading "Welcome to Holland."
- Explain that the purpose of this group is to help parents recognize and accept their initial feelings about arriving in Holland, acclimate themselves to the change in plans and expectations, and, finally, appreciate how they may benefit from being where they are.

2. Ask the group what they know about parenting:

- Where and how did you learn to be a parent?
- What familiar sayings did you hear from your parents?
- What did you learn from those sayings about the role of children? How did you feel about them?
- How did your parents' rules fit their culture? Why might some of their rules not fit today's culture?

    *Note: Most of us think our parents did a great job, so we do exactly as they did, or we think they did a poor job, so we do the opposite. This program challenges participants to become more conscious parents, to think more clearly about the goals of parenting and how to achieve them. There may be some better options to choose from, rather than doing exactly as our parents did or doing the opposite.*

3. Define the goals of parenting: Ask the group to identify the qualities they hope their child will develop. List these as parents generate them. Allow plenty of time for this list to evolve. Generally, you will have to add very little. If the group seems stuck, ask the members to think about the skills that are necessary for successful adults in this culture.

    Have parents record the final list of qualities on page 15 in their guidebooks.

    *Note: The qualities on this list become the "destinations" on the parenting journey, the places we want our children to go.*

4. Ask group members: "Now that we know where we want our children to go, how do we help them get there? What qualities make a good parent?"

▶ List their answers.

▶ When the list is complete, have parents record it in their guidebooks on pages 15 and 16.

*Note: The group will probably quickly observe that the same characteristics they have listed as qualities for children will describe healthy parents. Take them a step beyond this by asking exactly what actions a parent must take with a child to develop those characteristics. Examples will include such things as being a good listener, being tolerant, having a sense of humor, taking time for self-care, being encouraging of others, and so on. This list becomes the "road map," the ways we guide our children to reach their destinations.*

5. Ask the group members what they think gets in the way of practicing all these "good parent" skills. Ask participants to look at the list of feelings that you developed previously about arriving in Holland when they wanted to be in Italy. How might having those feelings interfere with performing the tasks of effective parenting?

6. Set personal goals for the class. Do a round in which each participant refers to the list of qualities that make a good parent. Invite each parent to identify one parenting skill that he or she performs well now and one parenting skill he or she would like to improve on during the program. Have each person make a note of these skills. (Some parents may need prompting to help with the self-approval portion of this task.)

7. If time allows, have each parent identify one item from the list of qualities they hope their child will develop. Have them rate, on a scale of 0 to 10, where they feel the child is functioning in this category today.

*Note: Let the group know that the idea of scaling suggests that most children can be successful to some degree in developing these qualities and that the goals for the group will be to plan how to help children improve themselves in these areas. The goal is not perfection (to have a 10 every time). For example, a child may be somewhat respectful (5), rarely independent (2), or often responsible (8). In other words, help the participants identify the goals of parenting and encourage them to applaud growth, rather than noticing only perfection, both in themselves and in their children.*

# CLOSING

1. Express appreciation for the effort parents are making and for their willingness to share themselves with the group.

2. Let the parents know that what they will receive from the group will be in proportion to what they put into it, so it is important for them to read and complete activities for chapter 2 in the *Parent Guidebook* before the next meeting. They should also read the full text of chapter 1.

3. Refer parents to the interactive family activities on page 19 in their guidebooks. Remind the parents that the program is family based and reinforce the need to complete these activities as a family. If a family cannot or chooses not to complete a particular activity, it may substitute another one, but the family is expected to begin to spend more time together and to be together in a positive way. Each succeeding session will open with discussion on how the family activity went.

4. Ask if everyone plans to attend the following session.

   *Note: It is a good idea to ask this question at the end of each session in order to plan for child care and group continuity.*

# CHAPTER 2
# LISTENING TO OURSELVES

## OBJECTIVES

1. Identify personal hopes, dreams, and expectations about becoming a parent.
2. Identify differences between hopes, dreams, and expectations and the reality of parents' situations.
3. Identify feelings that may accompany the loss of hopes, dreams, and expectations.
4. Build group rapport and empathy.

## MATERIALS

Name tags, pencils or pens

Prepared posters of the lists created in Session 1: desired qualities in children and desired qualities in parents

Drawing paper and art supplies

*Greet all participants and hand out name tags again. Give any new group members a name tag to fill out. Use tags until parents know one another by first name. Make arrangements for any parents who have not taken the pretest to do so.*

## INTRODUCTION

1. Welcome participants back and introduce any new members. (We do not recommend accepting new members after this session.)
2. Ask group members to share their experience with the interactive family activities for the previous session.
3. Ask the members how many made time to read and complete the material for chapters 1 and 2 in the *Parent Guidebook*.
4. Refer the group to the lists of qualities parents hope their child will develop and qualities they feel make a good parent, created during the last session. Briefly explain to new members that

these are the destinations list and road map for the group's journey.

## SESSION PLAN

1. Complete a round in which parents describe their interaction with their children as a dance form. Which one is it (for example, a waltz, hip-hop, tango)? Who is leading, and who is following?

2. Do a second round in which group members share something a parent did or said when they were children that they promised not to say or do to their own children. Ask if they have been successful in avoiding this behavior with their children.

3. Do a third round: Have parents share what the biggest surprise has been about being a parent. What is most different from what they expected? (Answers should focus on expectations about parenting, not on the special needs of the child.)

4. Invite parents to draw a picture of their family with all members performing some activity. Tell the group that they will share their drawings but that the drawings will not be judged by the quality of the artwork and that no criticism of the content will be offered. Distribute the drawing paper and art supplies and allow about 15 minutes for each person to complete the drawing.

   *Note: Adults may be very uncomfortable the first time they are asked to complete an art activity in the group. Remind them that each time a child is given a new task, he or she may have some of these same feelings. Ask adults to think about what helps to encourage children to risk trying new activities. It is very important that facilitators participate in art activities and, as time allows, share their own drawings. Doing so models how parents can be more supportive of their children's efforts to take risks.*

5. Have each group member share his or her drawing with the group and explain who is in the family and what each person is doing, then have each member explain what he or she likes and dislikes about the family. After each person has commented, encourage participants to ask questions or make observations. Remind them to refrain from commenting on artistic skill.

6. Refer to the two vignettes on pages 25 and 26 of the *Parent Guidebook,* about Miguel and Laura. Read them aloud. Ask the parents to identify some of the feelings that Miguel and Laura might be experiencing. How will their feelings affect how they treat their children?

7. Ask each parent to identify the trait in their child that pleases them the most and the trait that disappoints them the most. Assist the parents in deciding why this is so. Ask:

   ► Which of your expectations have been met, and which ones have been thwarted?

   ► What feelings accompany this loss in what you expected from your child?

   ► How do these feelings affect the way you discipline or behave toward your child?

8. Refer to the discussion about parents' difficult feelings in acknowledging their dreams and expectations. Underscore the idea that the group is about accepting one's feelings about having a child with special needs—all the feelings.

   *Note: Parents may need help to understand that feelings are not good or bad, right or wrong. They may be painful or pleasant. You may need to identify the four general categories of feelings (mad, sad, glad, scared) at this time. Many adults will talk about thoughts rather than feelings, and you will need to gently redirect the discussion toward feelings at this point.*

## CLOSING

1. Thank participants for taking the time to attend and allow an opportunity for final comments or questions.

2. Remind the group of the need to do the reading and interactive family activities for chapter 3 to prepare for the next meeting.

3. Ask whether everyone plans to return to the group for the following session.

# CHAPTER 3
# LISTENING TO OUR CHILDREN

## OBJECTIVES

1. Identify personal losses.
2. Understand the grieving process as emotional healing.
3. Identify specific impact on family of having a child with special needs.
4. Begin to recognize emotional boundaries between parent and child.

## MATERIALS

Drawing paper and art supplies

## INTRODUCTION

1. Welcome participants back to the group.
2. Ask group members to share their experience with the interactive family activities during the previous session.
3. Ask group members how they made time to complete the material in the guidebook.
4. Allow time for questions or thoughts arising from the previous session.

## SESSION PLAN

1. Conduct a round: Ask group members to share in a little more detail the nature of each child's special needs, being specific about when they learned about the problems. Keep this round brief, as its purpose is to set the stage for the next activity.
2. Distribute drawing paper and art supplies and ask parents to draw a picture of how they felt when they first found out that their child had a special need. The drawing may be abstract or realistic.

3. Share drawings among group members. Follow the suggestions in the note on page 26 in this book for processing drawings.

   *Note: Be prepared for this to be an emotional experience for some group members. Remember to model active listening in order to help members identify the feelings they may be experiencing currently as well as at the time of loss, rather than letting them focus on events such as experiences in a medical setting or at school.*

4. Conduct another round: Encourage group members to identify what their child may be feeling about being "special." How do they know this is what the child is feeling?

   *Note: You are beginning to set the stage for Session 5, when parents will think about understanding a child's behavior and helping the child learn the words to express feelings. More important, you are also beginning to teach parents to recognize that what they imagine a child to be feeling and what the child is actually feeling may not be the same. This ties into the portion of the previous session on boundaries. An important boundary for parents to recognize is that a child's feelings may be very different from the parents'.*

5. Help parents understand that in a healthy family, children are not expected to meet the needs of the adults. Refer to the list of qualities desirable for healthy children created in the first session. Ask parents to identify which of these qualities would require a parent to model healthy boundaries. (Respect, responsibility, self-control, and independence should be noted in particular.)

6. Encourage parents to identify some healthy boundaries inside the family, such as the right to privacy, which could be reflected by knocking before entering someone's room, children's not listening at their parents' bedroom door, parents not going through children's possessions without permission, and so on.

## CLOSING

1. Allow for final comments or questions.
2. Refer parents to their guidebooks to note the interactive family activities. Observe that, from the activities described the one that will be the most informative is the second suggestion, involving observing the child's interaction with someone else. Urge parents to take time to do this activity, even though it may be difficult.

# CHAPTER 4

# HOW DO WE HEAL?
# IS IT OK TO CRY?

## OBJECTIVES

1. Recognize differences in styles of processing loss as learned in families of origin.
2. Recognize commonalities and differences in the way parents experience the intense feelings that accompany a loss.
3. Identify special difficulties encountered in the chronic grieving process.
4. Identify impact of the grieving process on parenting tasks.

## MATERIALS

DVD or videotape and player *(optional)*

Drawing paper and art supplies

## INTRODUCTION

1. Welcome parents back to the group.
2. Check in on parents' experiences with the interactive family activities. Ask them to share what they learned from watching their child. Were they able to identify their child's feelings based upon the behavior they observed?

   *Note: This activity will continue to prepare parents for Session 5.*

## SESSION PLAN

1. If possible, show parents part of a DVD or video of a film depicting how parents respond very differently to a loss associated with their child. For example:

- In *Lorenzo's Oil,* Lorenzo's parents argue about whether to continue treatment.

- In *Parenthood,* the mother and father disagree about the seriousness of their son's social ineptitude.

- In *Angie,* Angie and her family experience the birth of a child with an incompletely formed arm.

  *Note: If you are unable to show a film clip, parents are likely to have seen films that illustrate this point and can identify and describe scenes in which parents' responses are at odds. Not all parents need to have seen a particular film for this retelling to be effective.*

2. Focus on understanding where we learned about the intense feelings that accompany loss and how we express these feelings.

   - Have group members draw a picture that depicts an early loss in their lives. (The loss might not have been a death. It could have been your parents' divorce, a move, a friend moving, etc.). Ask them to think about how others around them treated their loss and how they did or didn't express their feelings.

   - When they have finished, have group members share their drawings. Have the group identify and discuss their families' rules for grieving. Emphasize the differences in how different families and cultures grieve.

3. Refer parents to their guidebooks to review the material on anger. Discuss the relationship between anger and loss and encourage the group to give examples of ways that adults can express anger appropriately.

   *Note: The discussion on anger is a good time for you to identify families in which the expression of anger is out of control and to refer them for individual or family therapy. By now, enough trust may have been established in the group that such suggestions can be offered with sensitivity.*

4. Help group members recognize how chronic grieving may be different from grieving for a specific loss:

   - Invite group members to share their experiences with chronic grieving.

   - Ask members to brainstorm what a person in a state of chronic grief needs to do in order to soothe herself or himself.

   - How does the state of chronic grieving alter parenting tasks? Ask parents to be specific in identifying the effect of grieving on optimal parenting.

*Note: Draw the group's attention to the fact that all of the feelings associated with the grieving process might also be described in general as feeling "out of control." Ask the group to think about how a parent's personal emotional experience might impact parenting: What do parents generally do when they feel out of control? Answers should include the idea that they try to control what they feel is the source of their pain—the child. In other words, parents typically attempt to control external events related to their feelings, rather than searching for ways to manage those feelings internally. Generally, this response leads to an escalation in the child's challenging behavior since children mirror their parents' emotional state.*

## CLOSING

1. Refer to the interactive family activities in the guidebook. Help parents begin to think about the first activity, in which they design an experiment in handling their child's behavior in a different way. Let parents know you will be following up on this activity during the next session.

2. Ask parents to create a family activity of their own before the next session.

3. Allow time for questions, comments, and wrap-up.

# CHAPTER 5

# UNDERSTANDING OUR CHILDREN

## OBJECTIVES

1. Begin to develop the skill of active listening and apply this skill to listening to feelings.
2. Develop understanding of how to read a child's behavior as a guide to identifying the feeling behind it.
3. Apply understanding of the feelings/behavior relationship to the child's specific behaviors at home.

## MATERIALS

None

## INTRODUCTION

1. Welcome parents back to the group.
2. Ask parents to share the family activity they created and tried out since the past session. (Having parents share gives other parents ideas about new activities to consider.) Be sure to identify how each family modified its activity to include the child with special needs.
3. Postpone discussion of the activity involving changing the child's challenging behavior until later in the session.
4. Ask parents to discuss any additional thoughts they might have about the last session's topic of loss and grieving.

## SESSION PLAN

1. Set up a role play based on the example in the *Parent Guidebook* involving Alexander and his baseball card collection (p. 55).

   ► Have one parent volunteer to play Alexander and another to play his parent. Have them act out the scene as it might really occur at home. Then have the group make observations or give suggestions about how the parent could relate differently to Alexander.

> Review "How to Listen" in the guidebook (pp. 54–55).

> Have the actors try the scene again, applying active listening skills.

2. Divide the group into dyads. (Parenting partners should not work together.) Have the partners take turns completing the sentence "One thing that angers me about my family is _____ ." The listeners should practice active listening skills to draw out the speakers and to help the speakers generate some possible solutions to the problem without giving any advice.

3. Take a few minutes to process the experience in the larger group.

4. Refer to the vignettes about David (p. 52) and Alexander and review information on feelings and acting-out behaviors of children.

*Note: To point out the importance of teaching children how to verbalize their feelings, remind parents of the intricate communication system between primary care-taker and child in the early months of life. Most parents will readily agree that they could distinguish differences in their baby's crying and understand what the baby was feeling or needed very early in the infant's life. Verbalizing helps children feel in control of themselves and can take the place of acting out.*

5. Return to the interactive family activities from the previous session. Ask parents how their new responses to handling their child's behavior are working. If time allows, invite the group to help problem-solve with those parents who are frustrated with the results. Encourage parents to continue to practice changing their behaviors.

*Note: Remind parents that what they are modeling for their children is that it is OK to learn from mistakes and that parents are also continuing to grow.*

## CLOSING

1. Review the interactive family activities for this session.

*Note: The purpose of the first activity is to help parents recognize the feelings that may trigger a child's acting-out behaviors and help parents begin to respond to those feelings rather than automatically punishing the behavior in hopes of eliminating it. It is also designed to help parents recognize their own feelings as they respond to their children's behaviors. Sometimes parents' feelings prevent them from making wise decisions about discipline.*

2. Invite comments, questions, and discussion of any unfinished business.

# CHAPTER 6

# EMPOWERING OURSELVES AND OUR CHILDREN

## OBJECTIVES

1. Understand and apply appropriate expectations based on the developmental level of the child.
2. Recognize and plan how to support the emotional needs of the special child, who may be grieving the loss of physical functioning or normalcy in other areas.
3. Recognize parenting pitfalls, overprotectiveness, and power struggles, and apply general parenting principles to the child with special needs.
4. Encourage supportive exchange of problem-solving ideas between parents.
5. Identify goals for improved family functioning.
6. When a children's group is being conducted, provide parents with alternative perceptions about their children.

## MATERIALS

None

## INTRODUCTION

1. Welcome parents back to the group.
2. Ask parents to identify any ways they see that a child may be expressing his or her own feelings about losing something important.

   *Note: Parents often have difficulty letting a child express feelings because the process is painful to them. Facilitators need to remind parents to think about what helps them express and cope with their own feelings. Some parents will see denial and avoidance as the only possible responses to strong feelings. If they teach (model) those responses to their children, they will have children who will continue to act out their feelings in inappropriate or disruptive ways. Again, we are talking about boundaries—parents' ability to tolerate the fact that their children may feel differently than they do.*

## SESSION PLAN

1. Encourage discussion of the information in the *Parent Guidebook* on children's developmental stages. Have parents consider the relationship between their child's chronological and emotional age, based on the child's behaviors. For example, a parent may have an eight-year-old who has temper tantrums, cannot delay gratification, and exhibits little responsibility. Emotionally, the child is behaving like a two-year-old. Have parents assess whether the child has developed to an optimal level. Are these delays actually due to the child's special need, or are some of the emotional delays the result of parenting style? Some children who are cognitively challenged, for example, may be capable of developing emotionally on a rather normal schedule.

2. Refer to Danny's situation in the guidebook (p. 72). Ask parents to brainstorm appropriate parenting interventions for this situation. How does the fact that Danny is emotionally two years old impact parenting? What needs to be considered?

3. Refer to Emma's situation in the guidebook (pp. 74–75). Encourage a discussion among parents based on the questions following the vignette.

   *Note: By now parents should be expressing some of their own limitations and identifying areas they would like to change. Group members should be able to help one another accept that some of their parenting problems occur because they feel guilty about or sorry for their children and, as a result, don't apply appropriate interventions, such as consequences for misbehavior. Children with special needs usually do not need to rule a family emotionally because of their special situation, yet sometimes they are allowed to do so, often to the great injustice of other children in the family. Help parents look at their own feelings and how they get in the way of parenting.*

4. Refer to Jason's situation, on page 35 of the guidebook. Encourage a discussion among parents based on the questions following the

vignette. Emphasize the meaning of overprotection as noted in the vignette.

*Note: Some parents are very defensive about being overprotective. Refer to the list the group made during its first session in which it identified characteristics it would like to foster in children. Ask if overprotectiveness is allowing the child to develop to the optimal level. Remind group members that children want to be treated normally and need to be given as much responsibility as possible.*

5. Spend time with parents as they discuss ways they have and have not used effective interventions with their children. Encourage them to describe their experiences in as much detail and with as much objectivity as possible, then ask the group to help individual parents think about other and possibly more effective interventions.

6. Review any noteworthy progress each parent or child has made based on the lists of goals established for children and parents from the first session.

## CLOSING

1. Review the interactive family activities. The second activity is particularly important because it requires the family to work together in visualizing the ideal family.

2. Allow time for comments, questions, and discussion of unfinished business.

# CHAPTER 7
# CELEBRATING OUR CHILDREN

## OBJECTIVES

1. Identify optimal growth potential in the child with special needs.
2. Problem-solve parents' applications of the specific skills necessary to reduce dependency and foster growth in the child.
3. Identify and share areas of joy and hope that parents are experiencing in relating to their child with special needs.

## MATERIALS

None

## INTRODUCTION

1. Welcome parents back to the group.
2. Invite group members to share their experience with the family activities they tried after the last session.
3. Ask group members to share their continuing observations of interactions in the home:

   ► What behaviors did they observe in their child with special needs since the last session, and what feelings do they believe the child was acting out through these behaviors?

   ► Ask the group to help one another explore how they might handle these situations better, if they did not go well.

## SESSION PLAN

1. Focus discussion on understanding what arriving in Holland instead of Italy means and how the pain of certain experiences can be transforming. Work with the group to generate examples and help them express the idea that "I didn't think I could stand the pain, but I did, and I now value the experience." Help them see the possibility that as we let go and admit our losses, we open

to new and often inspiring gains. Refer parents to page 85 in the guidebook.

> ► Conduct a round: Have each participant complete the following sentence as applied to his or her child with special needs:
>
> "I appreciate my child's _____ ."
>
> ► Conduct another round: Have each participant complete the following sentence as applied to being the parent of a child with special needs:
>
> "I appreciate myself for _____ ."

2. Discuss the ways parents responded to the questions that follow in the guidebook about how having a child with special needs has affected family priorities, the experience of love, the demands of advocacy, spirituality, and siblings.

3. Apply the "optimal child" concept to the specific children with special needs represented in this group by having a parent describe a situation involving the child in which the parent encounters frustration. Have the parent explain in some detail what the child does or says so the group has a clear idea of the problem. If appropriate to the group, role-play the scene by having parents play different members of the family.

4. Complete as many role plays as time allows. After each one, encourage the group to provide helpful feedback to the parents who suggested the situations.

## CLOSING

1. Look at the interactive family activities for the session. Think with parents about how to create an "Appreciation Day" for their children and for themselves.

2. Invite comments, questions, and discussion of unfinished business.

3. Remind participants that the next meeting will be the last one.

# CHAPTER 8

# BEING A CONSCIOUS PARENT

## OBJECTIVES

1. Practice acceptance of loss through the expression of feelings.
2. Develop the ability to express appreciation for self and others.
3. Set goals for future growth in parenting skills.
4. Provide evaluation and feedback to facilitators.

## MATERIALS

Refreshments for the group to share

Collage materials: paper, magazine pictures and words, marking pens, crayons, glitter, glue, and fabric scraps or trims

Small squares of paper

Copies of the Pretest-Posttest (Appendix A), Program Evaluation (Appendix B), and Certificate of Attendance (Appendix C)

## INTRODUCTION

1. Welcome parents back to the group.

   *Note: Because the experiences of the group should not be rushed, we suggest putting the refreshments out at the beginning and letting parents snack throughout the activities.*

2. Invite parents to share their thoughts about having an Appreciation Day for their children.

3. Allow some time for parents to discuss how their efforts to change their parenting style are working. Ask if they have used new skills they learned in the group.

   *Note: Remind parents of the need for consistency. They are practicing new skills and must remain patient and avoid making assumptions about whether or not the skills will work. They are also modeling for children the persistence it takes to learn new skills and the self-esteem that results.*

## SESSION PLAN

1.  Remind parents that having a child with special needs means saying good-bye to expectations, to dreams, and to "Italy." Only after we say good-bye to those expectations can we truly acknowledge what is to be gained from this unexpected experience. This final session is designed to help parents say good-bye in a healthy way.

2.  Have each group member separately create a collage made from materials you provide. Explain that the collage is to depict something about how each person says hello and good-bye. Allow about 20 minutes for parents to complete their collages.

    *Note: It is best if the group works in silence so that each person gets in touch with her or his own experience.*

3.  After parents have finished their collages, conduct a round to share them. Invite parents to describe what the collages mean. Keep this round brief and follow the guidelines for noncritically discussing the artwork.

4.  Provide a packet of small squares of paper for each parent and facilitator. Give parents enough time to write a note of appreciation to each person in the group. After everyone has finished writing, and if parents are willing, have them take turns reading these notes of appreciation aloud. If there is not enough time to do this, make sure that each parent receives the comments from other group members before leaving.

5.  Use the change process suggested in the *Parent Guidebook* to help parents develop specific plans to continue the work they have been doing in class.

## CLOSING

1.  Remind parents to continue spending time doing family activities.

2.  Encourage parents to continue becoming more conscious of their skills as parents. If available, other parenting classes or groups might help them continue to work toward their goals. Encourage them to check out the resources suggested at the end of the Parent Guidebook and refer them to our Web site: interactivefamilyresources.com.

    *If parents have experienced some emotional release during this program, they will be more receptive to more task-oriented parenting classes and more able to adapt the information presented to their particular situations.*

3. Have parents complete the Pretest-Posttest and the Program Evaluation.

4. Present each participant with a Certificate of Attendance. Congratulate parents for their hard work during the program.

# APPENDIXES

# APPENDIX A: RAISING SPECIAL KIDS PRETEST-POSTTEST

Name _____ Date _____

*Instructions: Circle the number that most accurately and honestly represents what is currently true in your life.*

| | Strongly disagree | Disagree | Sometimes agree/ sometimes disagree | Agree | Strongly agree |
|---|---|---|---|---|---|
| 1. When I have a question about my child with special needs, I know whom to contact or where to go for an answer. | 1 | 2 | 3 | 4 | 5 |
| 2. I think it is OK to feel sad, angry, or scared about having a child with special needs. | 1 | 2 | 3 | 4 | 5 |
| 3. I understand how my child's feelings affect his/her behavior. | 1 | 2 | 3 | 4 | 5 |
| 4. When my child is misbehaving, I know how to respond. | 1 | 2 | 3 | 4 | 5 |
| 5. I have been able to talk with others about my deepest feelings about having a child with special needs. | 1 | 2 | 3 | 4 | 5 |
| 6. I am happy with how I parent my child with special needs. | 1 | 2 | 3 | 4 | 5 |
| 7. It is easier to see my child's limitations than his/her potentials. | 1 | 2 | 3 | 4 | 5 |
| 8. Our family has clearly stated rules about what behaviors are and are not acceptable. | 1 | 2 | 3 | 4 | 5 |
| 9. I encourage my child with special needs to express his/her feelings. | 1 | 2 | 3 | 4 | 5 |
| 10. Sometimes I feel like no one else understands what it is like to have a child with special needs. | 1 | 2 | 3 | 4 | 5 |
| 11. I am unable to discipline my child/children without losing my temper. | 1 | 2 | 3 | 4 | 5 |
| 12. I am aware of the impact that having a child with special needs has had on me, my partner, and my other children. | 1 | 2 | 3 | 4 | 5 |
| 13. I can say no to my child with special needs without feeling guilty. | 1 | 2 | 3 | 4 | 5 |

From *Raising Special Kids: A Group Program for Parents of Children with Special Needs (Facilitator's Manual),* by Jared D. Massanari and Alice E. Massanari, © 2008, Champaign, IL: Research Press (800-519-2707, www.researchpress.com)

| | Strongly disagree | Disagree | Sometimes agree/ sometimes disagree | Agree | Strongly agree |
|---|---|---|---|---|---|
| 14. I know my child's strengths. | 1 | 2 | 3 | 4 | 5 |
| 15. I have accepted that I may have to alter some of the hopes and dreams I had for my child with special needs. | 1 | 2 | 3 | 4 | 5 |
| 16. I know very few parents who are raising children with special needs. | 1 | 2 | 3 | 4 | 5 |
| 17. It is inappropriate to grieve about having a child with special needs. | 1 | 2 | 3 | 4 | 5 |
| 18. My entire family spends time together each week having fun. | 1 | 2 | 3 | 4 | 5 |
| 19. I am not sure what stages my child might go through as he/she develops. | 1 | 2 | 3 | 4 | 5 |
| 20. I have rarely been given advice about parenting that directly relates to my situation as a parent of a child with special needs. | 1 | 2 | 3 | 4 | 5 |
| 21. I believe that the way my parents raised me has affected the way I raise my child/children. | 1 | 2 | 3 | 4 | 5 |
| 22. I find myself yelling a lot to control my child/children. | 1 | 2 | 3 | 4 | 5 |

# Pretest-Posttest Scoring Sheet

*To score the pretest and posttest, respectively, total the numbers each participant circles.* **Please note, however, that questions 13, 14, 21, 24, and 25 are scored in the reverse; that is, a circled 1 is added as a 5, 2 becomes a 4, 3 is a 3, 4 is a 2, and 5 is a 1.** *Following this procedure enables an accurate comparison of total score on the pretest with the cumulative total on the posttest.*

|  | Pretest | Posttest | Percent of change |
|---|---|---|---|
| Participant 1 | _____ | _____ | _____ |
| Participant 2 | _____ | _____ | _____ |
| Participant 3 | _____ | _____ | _____ |
| Participant 4 | _____ | _____ | _____ |
| Participant 5 | _____ | _____ | _____ |
| Participant 6 | _____ | _____ | _____ |
| Participant 7 | _____ | _____ | _____ |
| Participant 8 | _____ | _____ | _____ |
| Participant 9 | _____ | _____ | _____ |
| Participant 10 | _____ | _____ | _____ |
| Participant 11 | _____ | _____ | _____ |
| Participant 12 | _____ | _____ | _____ |

*Calculate the percent of change by dividing the total score of the pretest by 110 (total score possible on 22 questions), dividing the total score on the posttest by 110, then subtracting the pretest score from the posttest score. For example: Participant 1 has a total score of 88 on the pretest and 95 on the posttest.*

| Pretest | Posttest | Percent of change |
|---|---|---|
| $\frac{88}{100} = .80$ | $\frac{95}{110} = .86$ | $.06 = 6\%$ |

# APPENDIX B: RAISING SPECIAL KIDS PROGRAM EVALUATION

1. What did you find most beneficial about the program?

   _____

   _____

   _____

   _____

2. What are three things that you learned?

   a. _____

   b. _____

   c. _____

3. What would you recommend changing?

   _____

   _____

   _____

   _____

4. *(If your children participated)* What did your children like/dislike about their group?

   _____

   _____

   _____

   _____

# Certificate of Attendance

has completed the

## Raising Special Kids

*Parenting Program*

Sponsored by _____

Date _____

_____
Facilitator

_____
Facilitator

From *Raising Special Kids: A Group Program for Parents of Children with Special Needs (Facilitator's Manual)*, by Jared D. Massanari and Alice E. Massanari, © 2008, Champaign, IL: Research Press (800-519-2707, www.researchpress.com)

# RESOURCES

## Books and Articles

Bluebon-Langner, Myra. (1996). *In the Shadow of Illness: Parents and Siblings of the Chronically Ill Child.* Princeton, NJ: Princeton University Press.

Bowlby, John A. (1988). *Secure Base: Parent-Child Attachment and Healthy Human Development.* New York: Basic Books.

Brazelton, T. Berry, & Greenspan, Stanley. (2000). *The Irreducible Needs of Children: What Every Child Must Have to Grow, Learn, and Flourish.* New York: Perseus Publishing.

Clubb, Roni. (1991). Chronic Sorrow: Adaptation Patterns of Parents with Chronically Ill Children. *Pediatric Nursing,* September/October, *17*(5), 461–466.

Crane, Sam. (2003). *Aiden's Way.* Naperville, IL: Sourcebooks.

Crosse, Scott; Kaye, Elyse; & Ratnofsky, Alexander. (1992). *A Report on the Maltreatment of Children with Disabilities.* Washington, DC: National Center on Child Abuse and Neglect.

Dinkmeyer, Don, & McKay, Gary. (1973). *Raising a Responsible Child: How to Prepare Your Child for Today's Complex World.* New York: Simon and Schuster.

Faber, Adele, & Mazlish, Elaine. (1974). *Liberated Parents, Liberated Children: Your Guide to a Happier Family.* New York: Avon Books.

Featherstone, Helen. (1980). *A Difference in the Family: Living with a Disabled Child.* New York: Penguin Books.

Finston, Peggy. (1990). *Parenting Plus: Raising Children with Special Health Needs.* New York: Viking Press.

Funk, David. (2002). *Love and Logic: Solutions for Kids with Special Needs.* Golden, CO: Love and Logic Press.

Glasser, Howard, & Easley, Jennifer. (1998). *Transforming the Difficult Child: The Nurtured Heart Aproach.* New York: Berkley Books.

Hendrix, Harville, & Hunt, Helen. (1997). *Giving the Love That Heals: A Guide for Parents.* New York: Pocket Books.

Kabat-Zinn, Myla, & Kabat-Zinn, Jon. (1997). *Everyday Blessings: The Inner Work of Mindful Parenting.* New York: Hyperion.

Klein, Stan, & Kemp, John. (Eds.). (2004). *Reflections from a Different Journey: What Adults with Disabilities Wish All Parents Knew.* New York: McGraw-Hill.

Lavin, Judith. (2001). *Special Kids Need Special Parents: A Resource for Parents of Children with Special Needs.* New York: Berkley Books.

Massanari, Alice, & Massanari, Jared. (2000). *Our Life with Caleb.* Asheville, NC: InterActive Family Resources, PLLC. (www.interactivefamilyresources.com)

Massanari, Jared. (1996). The Transforming Possibilities of the Unexpected. *The ACCH Advocate, 2*(2), 17–19.

May, James. (1992). *Circles of Care and Understanding: Support Programs for Fathers of Children with Special Needs.* Bethesda, MD: Association for the Care of Children's Health.

McBryde-Johnson, Harriet. (2003, February 16). Unspeakable Conversations. *The New York Times Magazine.*

McCollum, Audrey. (1981). *The Chronically Ill Child: A Guide for Parents and Professionals.* New Haven, CT: Yale University Press.

Meyer, Donald. (Ed.). (1995). *Uncommon Fathers: Reflections on Raising a Child with a Disability.* Bethesda, MD: Woodbine House.

Moses, Ken, & Kearney, Robert. (1995). *Transition Therapy: An Existentialist Approach to Facilitating Growth in the Light of Loss.* Evanston, IL: Resource Network.

Oe, Kenzaburo. (1995). *A Healing Family.* New York: Kodansha International.

Popkin, Michael. (1983). *Active Parenting Program.* Atlanta, GA: Active Parenting, Inc.

Renfro, Sharon. (2003). *I Didn't Know That! The Basic Ideas for Successful Relationships.* (Available from www.booklocker.com)

Schwab, Reiko. (1997). Parental Mourning and Children's Behavior. *Journal of Counseling and Development, 75,* 258–265.

Tatelbaum, Judy. (1980). *The Courage to Grieve: Creative Living, Recovery, and Growth through Grief.* New York: Harper and Row.

## Feature Films

*Fly Away Home*

*Hannah and Her Sisters*

*Kramer versus Kramer*

*Life as a House*

*Lorenzo's Oil*

*Mask*

*Miracle in Lane 2*

*The Miracle Worker*

*My Left Foot*

*Parenthood*

*Patch Adams*

*What's Eating Gilbert Grape?*

## Web Sites

Active Parenting Programs: www.activeparenting.com

InterActive Family Resources, PLLC: www.interactivefamilyresources.com

Love and Logic Parenting Programs: www.loveandlogic.com

Fathers' Network: www.fathersnetwork.org

The Nurturing Father's Program: www.nurturingfathers.com

The Continuum Concept of Parenting: www.continuum-concept.org

The Infant-Parent Institute: www.infant-parent.com

# ABOUT THE AUTHORS

JARED D. MASSANARI has a master's degree in counseling from Florida State University and a doctorate in religious studies from Syracuse University. He has taught at various colleges and been a therapist for over 25 years. Much of his counseling practice has been with children and families, specializing in working with families raising children with special needs. He has written numerous articles and resources on this topic.

ALICE E. MASSANARI has a master's degree in English from the University of New Orleans and a master's degree in social work from the University of South Florida. She has experience in teaching, business, counseling, and conducting workshop trainings.

In addition to writing this parenting program, Alice and Jared have facilitated many parent groups and presented at a variety of conferences. They are the parents of two children, Adrienne and Caleb. Caleb's short life is chronicled in their book *Our Life with Caleb,* available through their Web site, www.interactivefamilyresources.com. Alice and Jared currently live in Asheville, North Carolina, where they continue their counseling practices and their writing, most recently *Building a House Together: A Couple's Guide to Managing Their Relationship during the Construction Process* (www.buildingahousetogether.com).